## About the Author

She was completely focused on her career; she worked fourteen hours a day running her own business. She lived on microwaved meals and fast-food takeaways, until she got sick. Between the doctor's appointments, the operations and recoveries, she decided to make a drastic change. She started growing her own produce and cooking her mother's recipes. It was the best decision she ever made, because now she is fully recovered and she has more energy than ever.

Check! Grow It – Cook It - Eat It

**Lizzy Mae van Son**

Check! Grow It – Cook It - Eat It

Olympia Publishers
*London*

www.olympiapublishers.com
OLYMPIA PAPERBACK EDITION

Copyright © Lizzy Mae van Son 2023

The right of Lizzy Mae van Son to be identified as author of
this work has been asserted in accordance with sections 77 and 78 of the
Copyright, Designs and Patents Act 1988.

**All Rights Reserved**

No reproduction, copy or transmission of this publication
may be made without written permission.
No paragraph of this publication may be reproduced,
copied or transmitted save with the written permission of the publisher, or in
accordance with the provisions
of the Copyright Act 1956 (as amended).

Any person who commits any unauthorised act in relation to
this publication may be liable to criminal
prosecution and civil claims for damage.

A CIP catalogue record for this title is
available from the British Library.

ISBN: 978-1-80439-397-0

This is a work of fiction.
Names, characters, places and incidents originate from the writer's imagination.
Any resemblance to actual persons, living or dead, is purely coincidental.

First Published in 2023

**Olympia Publishers
Tallis House
2 Tallis Street
London
EC4Y 0AB**

Printed in Great Britain

### Dedication

I dedicate this book to my amazing mother, Dymphy. If there was an award for best mother of the century, she would win it. She spends hours in the garden to grow fruits and vegetables, so that she could make homemade gourmet dishes for us.

**Acknowledgements**

Thank you to my brother, Philip, who cooked for me while I was writing and drawing this book.

"Nothing tastes better than your mother's love and effort put into a jar."
-Lizzy Mae van Son

This book is dedicated to my mother, to thank her for all the time she spent to care and love us. For the amazing knowledge that she passed on to me and my brother, not only in the garden but also in the kitchen. All the valuable life lessons that made sure that we would be safe on our journey in life. To the best mother on the planet, Dymphy van Son.

I am the usual millennial; Netflix and food deliveries in the evening and the occasional "healthy smoothie" during the day, to convince my mother that I am living healthy and taking care of myself. My mum knows all too well that in reality I am living off bags of chips and one-dollar hotdogs, due to my kitchen laziness and my stressful job. I run my own business, so eating comes in last place on my time schedule. For my business I travel a lot which of course doesn't help either, but the nice thing is that I am exposed to different cultures and their dishes.

A year ago, I started having health issues. I basically didn't have enough red blood cells so my organs were not getting enough oxygen. So I decided to take a break and move back home. It took a lot of doctor appointments and many pills until they found the cause, but what really helped me was my mum's home-cooked food. My mother loves gardening, and we have around forty different vegetables and fruits in our garden, which she uses to make her own recipes. Since we spent a lot of time together over this dark period, I started helping her out in the garden, by planting some tomatoes and leeks. I didn't expect it, but it was very enjoyable. One doctor told me that my condition would improve if I began to eat more healthily. My issue with cooking is that when I come home, I am generally exhausted and I don't want to spend another hour in the kitchen, preparing my dinner. Therefore, I decided to ask my mum to teach me some easy family recipes and I added a modern multicultural twist. This turned out to be the best decision ever – not only did my health improve, but I got to spend an amazing time with my mum. Throughout this book I will take you through each step, from planting your own produce to making something healthy and delicious with it.

# Sterilise to Avoid an Unwanted Surprise

Before we start with any recipes, you will need to know how to sterilise a jar or a bottle. This is necessary to make sure that there are no bacteria inside of your jars. If there are bacteria of some sort in your jars or bottles, then you will have mould in a short time, and will not be able to enjoy your products. You can buy glass bottles or jars at a local shop or you can recycle them, for example, pickles or spread jars.

The first thing you will have to do is to wash the jar and the lid thoroughly with dish soap, or if you have a dishwasher, you can let it do the job for you. Once they are clean, you will need to sterilise them, which is easier than it sounds. Put the jars or bottles on your oven tray with the lids next to each jar or bottle.

Put the tray in the oven and heat it up to 115 °C for ten minutes. While you are waiting for your jars, you can get started with a recipe. Once you are done with your recipe, take the jars out of the oven and fill it with your delicious recipe. Make sure to use kitchen mitts, close the lid and put your filled jars upside down for five minutes. After this, you have a product that you can store in a dark cupboard for a whole year, because it is sterilised. Now we can get started with the actual recipes.

# Strawberry Fun

Strawberries are little, low-calorie vitamin bombs, that also help protect your heart and lower your blood pressure.

**How to grow them:** Go to your local garden centre and buy a few strawberry plants. It doesn't matter if you have a balcony or a small garden, just put them in a pot (preferably in April or May.) Feed them with some extra fertiliser every two weeks and water them every day. They basically grow by themselves, and you will have your own strawberries from May to July.

Strawberry plants are also easy to propagate, so once you have one plant, you never have to buy more plants.

At a certain point you will see little lighter coloured knobs on your plants' stems – those are basically new plants. The only thing you need to do is to prepare a new small pot with soil and leave it close to your original strawberry pot, so that the stem with the nob can reach the new pot. Then with a hair or garden pin, you can pin the little nob down to the soil of the new pot, and leave the rest of the plant and leaves alone. The only thing is that the nob needs to touch the soil. You can leave the stem attached to the mother plant if you would like to harvest strawberries the same year. And within a year, you will have multiple strawberry plants.

**How to make Strawberry fun:** After you harvest your strawberries, or if you don't have the patience, you can also buy them in a store. Wash them by giving them a quick rinse with cold water. Then you have to cut off the crown (the green, leafy part) which you can throw on your compost. Cut the strawberries in 1 centimetre pieces, you don't need to be too precise.

Put all your cut pieces in a big bowl and check their weight. Add an equal amount of powdered sugar; for example, we had 1 kg of strawberries, so we put 1 kg of powdered sugar and add the juice of one lemon. Mix it with a spoon until you don't see any more white pieces of the powdered sugar. Cover the bowl and leave it for twelve hours in a cool and dark place.

The next day, start by putting a little plate in your freezer – you will understand later why. – and wash your jars thoroughly. You can buy jars in a store or just recycle some old jars you have left. You will also need to sterilise your jars, it sounds more complicated than what it is. Just put the jars in the oven with the lids next to each jar and heat it up to 115 degrees for ten minutes. While you are waiting for your jars Now you can start with your strawberries – put them in a sauce pan and heat up your mixture until it boils. Let it boil for fifteen to twenty minutes, until you reach the temperature of 104 °C. While it's boiling, you will see a pink foam forming on the top, which you can remove with a spoon and throw it away. When you like your consistency you can do the density test, to be sure that you will like the end result. Take the little plate out of the freezer and put a little bit of your strawberry fun on it. Wait a minute for the strawberry fun to cool off on your plate, and then, with your finger, you can touch the mixture to see if you like the density. If you find it too liquid then you need to boil it a bit more. If you are satisfied then you can take your jars out of the oven and fill them with your strawberries, make sure to use oven gloves since they will be very hot.

When you close the lid, put the jars upside down for ten minutes to rest and then turn them back to the normal jar position and let them cool off for a night. The next day your strawberry fun is ready to be used. You can store it in the kitchen cupboard for a year.

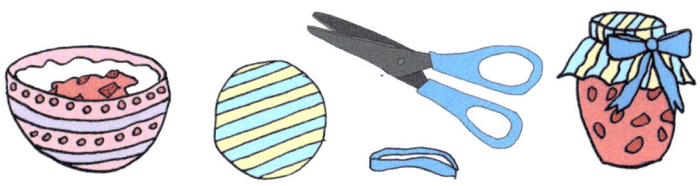

Different ideas for the strawberry fun: How to best use the strawberry fun depends a little on how dense it has become, depending on the altitude of where you live and the strength of your cooking stove, it can be or dense like a jam or a bit more liquid. If it is more liquid then open a Greek yoghurt and put a full spoon of strawberry fun on top, and you will have your own yoghurt-fruit mix that will taste so much better than any store-bought yoghurt. Or you can use it on top of a peanut butter sandwich and make it a peanut butter and jam sandwich. Our personal favourite is to use our strawberry fun as topping on a little ball of vanilla ice cream while we watch a movie together.

It also makes a great gift. Buy a piece of fabric that you like or use an old shirt and cut out a circle that is 4 or 5 centimetres bigger than the lid of your jar. Put it over the lid and use a ribbon to fix it and you will have your strawberry fun looking cute and ready to surprise your friends.

# Verbena Peace

Verbena has relaxing qualities for your mind and body. It will help you sleep better or recover from a stressful day. It also helps with stomach issues or cramps.

**How to grow it:** You can buy lemon verbena seeds, or just buy a small plant in a store. Plant it in a pot or in the garden and make sure you give it a sunny warm place. Verbena likes well-drenched soil, so you can water it every second day, and in hot summers, give it water every evening if you see the leaves go flat.

**How to use it:** You can make a fresh verbena tea. Just pick ten leaves off your plant, heat up water in your kettle, put the leaves in a tea glass and pour the water over it. Let the tea sit for three to five minutes so that the flavour can be absorbed by the water. You can drink it warm before going to bed to relax a little. To drink it cold, add a slice of lemon and you have a homemade ice tea. Another option is to cut off a few stems with leaves and hang them upside down in a dry place. Check every now and then if there is no moisture in between the leaves to avoid moulding.

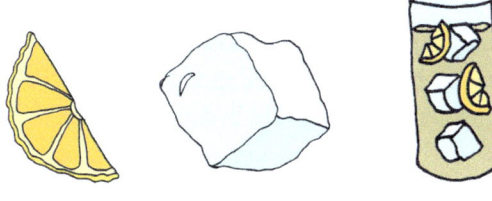

Once the leaves are completely dried you can take them off the stems and put them in a jar. You can leave the leaves like they are or if you prefer a real tea look, you can crumble them in between your hands. Now whenever you feel like having a verbena tea, your jar will be waiting for you.

# Basil Bonanza

If you suffer from high blood pressure issues, then basil can be your best friend. The essential oils of basil can help to lower cholesterol, and it also contains magnesium which can improve the blood flow by allowing the blood vessels and muscles to relax.

**How to grow it:** You can buy a little basil plant in any garden centre, and it's important to plant it in a bigger pot of around 15/20 centimetres in diameter. Put a piece of broken pot, if you have any, over the bottom hole of the pot so that the water doesn't drain too fast. Plant your basil in the pot. Now you need to give it a nice spot in the sun and make sure to water it daily if it is really hot, preferably in the evenings. Basil is quite easy, because the leaves will start hanging if it doesn't have enough water.

**How to harvest:** Cut the leaves of the upper parts of the basil plant so that your plant can regrow. The regrowth will take a few weeks.

**How to use it:** you can use basil in almost any dish, just put a few leaves on top as decoration, and your tomato spaghetti will look like it came straight from Italy. If you have more than one basil plant and therefore a lot of basil leaves, you can make fresh basil pesto. To make basil pesto you need to wash the leaves in a bowl of cold water and let them dry on kitchen paper. Put 3 spoons of olive oil and a clove of garlic in a mixer and mix it until you don't see the clove of garlic anymore. Then add the basil leaves in the mixer, together with 3 spoons of parmigiano cheese and a spoon of pine nuts if you like them, and mix it again. Now you have to go a bit by feeling and look at your pesto; you might need to add a bit more oil or a bit more leaves or cheese depending on the consistency. At the end you can also add some salt if it is needed. One you are satisfied with the look of your pesto you can put it on a bruschetta, toasted bread, or in your pasta.

Another thing you could make with basil is our basil bonanza which is a basil-infused olive oil which will give your salad an extra kick. In order to make the basil bonanza you need a litre of olive oil, basil leaves and a few empty glass bottles. You of course need to sterilise the bottles in advance, take the stems off your basil and delicately wash your leaves in a bowl of cold water. Let the leaves dry on kitchen paper to avoid any water drops.

Put the olive oil in a pan and heat it up to around 40 °C just to make it warm so that it absorbs the essential oils and aroma of the basil better. Once the oil is heated up you put all the leaves in your glass bottle or jar make sure you put as many leaves as you can, then you fill up your bottle or jar with the warm olive oil and close the lid. Make sure that all the leaves are covered by the oil. When you have all your bottles filled you need to put them in a dark kitchen cupboard and leave them there for three to four weeks. The only thing that you need to do is to turn them upside down each day, so that the aroma of the basil spreads to all the oil. One month later, you need to strain the leaves out of the oil and put the oil in a new sterilised bottle and you have a finished basil bonanza that you can use as a dressing for your salad. It's especially great on top of a caprese salad. You can keep your bottles for six months.

# Elderflower Power

Elderflower is a super healthy ingredient. It contains a lot of vitamins and antioxidants, and elderflower products help to prevent or cure influenza, sinusitis or other respiratory issues.

Where to find it: Elderflowers are widely spread all over the northern hemisphere. They are easily accessible because you can often find them next to the street, in the woods or in the occasional park. They are quite easy to recognise – it's a tree with mid-sized green leaves, and when they bloom in early May, they have bunches of little white flowers. In late August instead they produce elderberries, which are little black berries that are very poisonous if they are eaten raw. If you desire to use them you will first need to cook them.

**How to make Elderflower power syrup:** Take scissors and a bucket and put on some gardening boots. If you don't have a tree in your garden, take a walk around your neighbourhood and search for a tree with white flowers. When you have found a tree, cut the elderflowers off the tree until your bucket is full. You should only cut them if they are blooming, which is generally in early May. Once you are back in your kitchen, shake them out on a kitchen towel so that all the small insects drop on the towel. Don't be scared of the amount of tiny insects and don't be too worried if there are still some left. Proceed by removing the big stems and putting the flowers into a big bowl. Pour cold water over them until they're completely underwater. Cover it with a towel and leave it to rest for about twenty four hours in a cool and dark place.

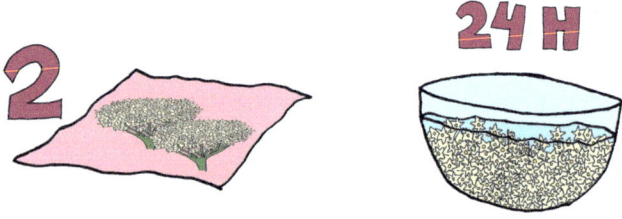

The next day, put a strainer on top of a cooking pot and put a clean dishcloth in the strainer, so that you strain out everything including the tiny insects. Pour your whole bowl of water and flowers into the strainer and wait till the liquid is in the pot and the flowers are in the dish cloth.

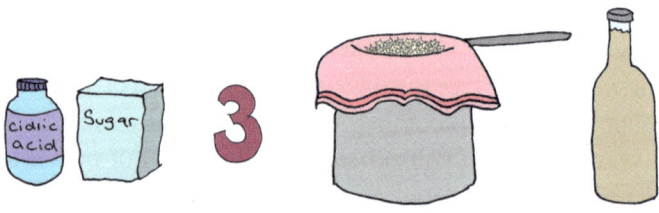

Measure the liquid – for every litre, you will need to add 20 grams of citric acid, which you can buy in any pharmacy, and 1100 grams of sugar. Then put it all in a pot and heat it on the stove for fifteen minutes and make sure that it doesn't boil. Once it reaches 98 °C you can put it in your sterilised bottles, fill them up till the top and close them immediately. Let them cool off and it's ready to be used. You can store it in your kitchen in a dark cupboard for a year, and once you open it you can leave it in the fridge for a month.

**How to use the syrup:** You can use it if you have a sore throat by just taking a spoon of the elderflower power, or you can put a little bit of the syrup in a glass and top it up with cold water, for a very healthy and refreshing summer drink. My twist was to put the syrup in a wine glass and to add a few mint leaves. I then topped it up with 50% prosecco and 30% sprite for the perfect summer hugo aperitivo time. My mum loved this new idea, but I am afraid that she thinks that I am an alcoholic now since I twisted every recipe into cocktail time.

# Dill Delicious

Dill is packed with flavonoids that can help reduce the risk of heart diseases and strokes. It also has great digestive qualities, by reducing the gas in your digestive system and avoiding a bloated feeling.

**How to grow it:** Buy a little dill plant at your local garden centre – they will be so thrilled to see you again! Buy some soil and a pot that is 20 centimetres wide and plant your dill. Let it grow till it is around 30 to 40 centimetres high before you harvest your dill.

**How to use it:** Once you have harvested your dill, you can use it fresh on almost any meal. It is especially delicious on top of a salmon and cream cheese sandwich. Another option is to let your dill dry, so that you can have dill for a whole year. Put your fresh cut dill on kitchen paper on a big plate or an oven tray, leave it on your window sill exposed to the natural sunlight for about two to three days until everything is dry. Now you can separate the small dill leaves from the bigger stems and put the small leaves into a clean jar. You can then have dill for a whole year on your sandwiches or inside your cucumber salads.

## Lavender Love

Lavender has a specific aroma that repels mosquitoes, and also prevents your clothes from being eaten by moths. The scent additionally helps to make you feel relaxed and sleep better.

**How to grow it:** Lavender is one of those flowers that you can find in any garden centre. They are also really easy to care for since they don't need much water and they survive well in a pot or you can plant it straight into the garden.

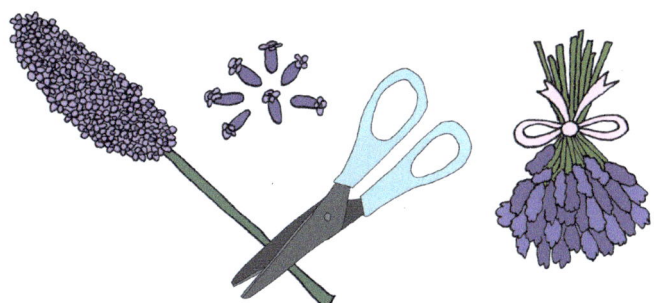

**How to use it:** Once you see that some of the buds start blooming with a tiny little purple flower, you can start to harvest them. The best is to harvest them right before they bloom. Cut the flowers off with normal scissors. The easiest is to leave 15 centimetres of stem so that you create a bundle of them and tie them together with a rubber band. Attach a paper clip to the rubber band and hang your flowers upside down in a dry place. Drying them will take around ten days depending on your climate.

After your lavender is completely dry you can separate the purple buds from the stem, which is super easy since they basically fall off themselves. Put the buds in a jar so that you can use them for cooking, or in a little bag so that you can put them in the closet. You can sew little bags by hand or with the sewing machine using an old shirt, or you can buy a fabric that you like for the occasion. Use the scissors to cut a rectangle of 7 by 18 centimetres. This will give you a little bag of the size of around 5 by 9 centimetres. You can of course also make them bigger or smaller. Fold the bag in half and let the outside of the bag look inwards so that you can sew the two sides and leave the top opening. When you have sown that together you can turn the bag inside out throughout the top opening. Use the top opening to fill your bag with the lavender buds and you can either close the top part with a ribbon, or by sewing it. And you will have a lovely bag to avoid your cashmere sweaters from being damaged, or a super thoughtful present to give to a friend.

# Pumpkin Power

There are different types of pumpkin or pumpkin-like vegetables. The best one to use to make a gourmet soup is butternut squash. Butternut squash is rich in important vitamins and disease-fighting antioxidants, which makes it the perfect ingredient for a cold winter night. It also has a very low-calorie amount, making it great if you want to lose those Christmas kilos.

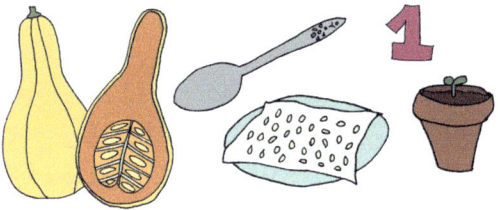

**How to grow it:** You can buy a butternut squash or a pumpkin in your local grocery store, so that you can straight away use it to for a cool recipe. While you slice the butternut squash in half, you will find the seeds. Use a spoon to remove the seeds, spread them on a kitchen paper supported by a plate and let them dry for a few days on a window sill. Once dried, you can remove the butternut seeds from the pulp by rubbing them in between your fingers until the seeds are clean. Once the seeds are clean you can roast them so that you have a healthy snack, or you can plant them. Put the seeds inside of a little pot with rich soil and give them lots of water. Leave the pot somewhere where it has a lot of warmth and sun. After a week you will see a green stem pop out of the pot; as soon as you see a few leaves you need to transfer it to a bigger pot, around 20 to 30 centimetres wide. If you start sowing it in January you will have big fresh butternut squash in September. When they turn dark yellow, they should be ripe and ready to be harvested. A little trick to know for sure that it's ripe is to knock on it with your finger, and if it sounds hollow then it means that it is ready to be harvested.

**How to use it:** Peel one butternut squash like you would peel an apple – cut it in half and take out the seeds. Cut the butternut into cubes of around 1 centimetre. Cut one onion in small pieces.

Put some oil in a cooking pan together with a tablespoon of mild curry, and add the onion, let the onion pieces turn a little brown and then add the butternut pumpkin. Stir it a bit and then add two cubes of vegetable stock in 1 litre of water and pour it into the pan.

Bring everything to the boiling point and switch the heat to medium and let it simmer for twenty minutes. Take a blender stick and puree everything till you have a creamy substance. Add salt, pepper and some hot chilli flakes if needed. Then you can put it in a bowl to have a lovely homemade meal. If you prefer something a little more fancy, you can add a spoon of cream on top and crumble an amaretto biscotti over it. It will add a more gourmet experience to it. The best part of the pumpkin power is that you can put it in a bag or a container and place it in the freezer, so that you will have it for three months whenever you need some strength during the cold winter times. Once you take it out of the freezer, just heat it up in the microwave or pan.

You can also eat the seeds. After you have cleaned and dried them, put the seeds on an oven tray and sprinkle a bit of salt on top and pour 2 to 3 spoons of olive oil over it. Put it in the oven for about fifteen to twenty minutes at 180 °C. The result will be lovely brown looking seeds that you can eat as a healthy snack.

## Hot Flakes

Adding some red pepper flakes to a dish will give it an extra kick and it will also help you digest or boost your immune system.

**How to grow it:** You can buy seeds of your chilly variety and sow them. With chilli peppers, it's important that they are not covered too much by soil, only a small layer is enough. Also make sure that they are covered by a plastic foil since the seeds only germinate when it's hot. It will take around ten days for you to see growth. They are also a very cute plant to have in your home since the peppers are so bright and joyful. You can also just buy a plant of a more common variety in the store.

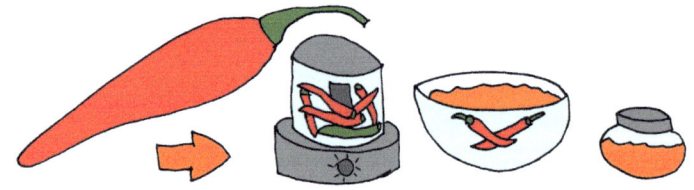

How to use it: It is very easy to make hot pepper flakes, but a little dangerous. Make sure to not touch your face after you have touched the peppers and wear a mask over your nose when you handle the pulverised pepper. It will sting if the flakes get in touch with sensitive body parts. Once you harvest your peppers you need to let them sun-dry, or the oven-dry. The easiest is to tie them together and hang them in the sun for a while. When your peppers are dried then you can put them in a blender and blend them until you have the flakes. Put the flakes in a bowl and add a spoon of oil and a pinch of salt. Now leave it in the sun for a day or two and keep stirring it with a spoon so that it all dries. After two days you are ready to put them in a spice jar.

# Tickle the Pickle

Cucumbers have any important vitamins and they have a really low caloric amount, so it's great to have in the garden for anyone that wants to lose some weight.

**How to grow it:** Buy cucumber seeds online or in a store. Once you have them at home, plant them in a small pot with rich soil. Bury the seeds 5 millimetres under the soil and give it lots of water. Cover the pot with a plastic pot cover or with transparent kitchen foil. Leave it in the sun so that the water condenses on to the covering and drops automatically back onto the soil. Once you see something green sticking out, you can remove the cover, and let the plant continue to grow by giving it water and sun daily. When your plant is around 10 centimetres tall you have to transfer it into a bigger pot, around 20 to 30 centimetre wide, so that it can continue to grow. Make sure it has a wall or chicken wire so that it can grow upwards. Give the cucumber plant lots of water in summer. If it is really hot and you see the leaves hanging, you can even water it twice a day. You will soon see yellow flowers that will be followed by cucumbers.

**How to use it:** Cucumbers are amazing because you can make so many things with it. Just cut it into pieces and eat it with your salad. I spend a lot of time abroad for work, so when we started planting cucumbers, I suggested that we try to make a Greek dip called tzatziki, which is a fresh yoghurt dip.

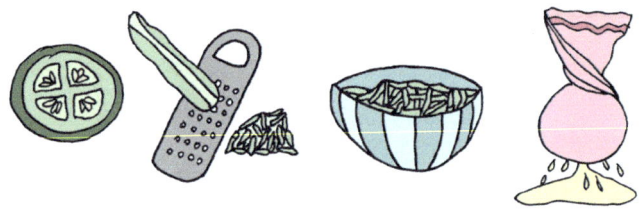

In order to make tzatziki you will need to peel the cucumber. Grate the peeled cucumber into thin long pieces and put it into a bowl, then add a pinch of salt and a spoon of white vinegar. Use a spoon to mix it all together and leave it aside while we get started with the yoghurt.

Put a half a clove of garlic into the mixer together with 3 spoons of olive oil. Mix it until it is one consistency, and you don"t see the garlic anymore. Put the yoghurt in a bowl together with your garlic olive oil and add a spoon of white wine vinegar, a pinch of salt and pepper, and mix it all together until it's creamy. Now you can take your cucumbers, put them in a dish towel and squeeze the cucumbers so that it will release all the liquid, so that when you add them to the yoghurt mixture it will stay creamy. When you add the cucumbers, you need to mix it in well, and for the finishing touch you need to mix in some dill. Now you can have a Greek lunch or dinner and use the tzatziki to dip your vegetables, your grilled meat or some bread.

Another option is to make your own pickles. Doesn't that sound amazing? It takes a little more time, but it's totally worth it. For pickles, it's best to use a smaller cucumber species. Or you can just buy the normal ones in the store and cut smaller pieces.

First you need to take out the seeds. The easiest is to slice the cucumber in half and then use a spoon to take them out, then cut it into 2 millimetres slices. We normally use around a kilo of cucumbers, but you can of course also use less.

Also chop an onion in fine slices, put them all in a bowl, add 3 spoons of salt and mix well. Cover the bowl with foil and let it sit for three hours. Come back every thirty minutes to mix it again and again. After three hours use a strain to take out the liquid, and rinse it well with water. Take a towel and squeeze the water out. Now your cucumbers are ready to be pickled. Put a pot on the stove and add 300 grams of brown sugar, 2 teaspoons of mustard seeds, 2 teaspoons of celery seeds and 1 teaspoon of turmeric. Of course, you can add more or less depending on your preferences. Then fill the pot with 1 litre of white wine vinegar and bring it to boil, once it boils switch it to medium for two minutes while stirring with a spoon. When the ingredients are well mixed, add the cucumbers and onion mixture and bring it to a boiling point again, while stirring every now and then. As soon as it boils again switch the stove off and you are ready to put your pickles in your sterilised jars. Make sure to use a strainer spoon so that you can first put the pickles in each jar, and then with a normal spoon you can top up the liquid, and add some fresh dill. Let it cool off and you will have your own pickles. You can keep the jars in a dark kitchen cabinet for a year, or if you open the jar, you can leave it in the fridge for a month.

## Berry Bubbles

All berries are like little vitamin bombs, there are different type of berries: blackberries, blueberries, raspberries, gooseberries, cranberry and many more variations and sub-variations. For example, there are a dozen different raspberries. But they have one thing in common, and that's that they are really healthy and delicious.

**How to grow it:** You can often find different types of berries in the woods, but be aware because some can also be very poisonous. If you are not sure that you can recognise the poisonous ones apart from the non-poisonous ones, you can just buy a little plant in a gardening centre and avoid the risk. In order to plant berries, you will need a bit more space since they can grow quite tall and they will need a growing support like a wall or a few poles connected by wire. You can plant your berries straight into your garden and water it daily during those hot summer days.

**How to use it:** If you don't have enough space in the garden or on your balcony, then you can buy your berries in the store. Berries can be used for so many different things: eat them as a snack, put them in your salad or in your yoghurt. If you have many berries that you can't eat all in one day, or you just want to make berry bubbles, then put your berries in a bowl of really cold water so that they don't become mush and take them out with a strainer so that they are clean.

Put your berries in a cooking pot and add an equal amount of powdered sugar. We had 250 grams of berries so we added 250 grams of powdered sugar. Then add 50 millilitres of water and half a lemon. Heat up the berries till they get very soft and let it simmer for ten minutes, but don't let it boil. When the berries are mush, strain the juice from the seeds into a new pot. You can use a spoon to push all the juices out of the fruit pulp. Now that you have the juice into a new pot, heat it up again and let it boil for a minute to get it a little more syrupy. Now it's ready and you can bottle it into your sterilised bottles. Now you must think that this is a simple juice. Well yes you can use it as such and dilute it with water, but you can also use it to sweeten your salad dressing.

In order to make a very unique berry bubble salad dressing you need to add 3 spoons of olive oil, 2 spoons of white vinegar, 1 spoon of mustard and 2 spoons of berry bubbles and mix it well till you have a very unique salad dressing. You can preserve the berry bubbles for four months in a dark kitchen cupboard and once opened you can keep it for a week in the fridge.

## Melon Madness

There are around forty melon types, the most common being the watermelon, the cantaloupe and the honeydew. Melons are really healthy – it doesn't matter which one you eat because they all improve your immune system.

**How to grow it:** It's very similar to planting pumpkin or cucumber. You can buy a melon in your grocery store and before eating it, you can remove the seeds, clean them and let them dry for a day or two. Then you can put your seed in a small pot, water it, and make sure you cover it with plastic foil or a special pot cover. After a few weeks, you should see your little melon plant grow out of the soil. Keep watering it daily, and leave it where it can have a full day of sun. When it is around 15 centimetres tall you need to repot it in a bigger pot. If you are also planting cucumbers, make sure to not confuse them, as they look quite similar. Don't leave the cucumber and melon too close to each other, or you might get a melon cucumber hybrid. Which, in my experience, was not too successful. A few summers ago, we made that mistake and the result was a dry, melon-looking cucumber.

**How to use it:** Slice the melon in half with a big knife and then use a spoon to remove the seeds, so that you can dry them and have them ready for the next planting time. Spoon half of the melon pulp out so that you can put it in a bag, which you can leave in the fridge for another day. The other half you can cut in slices and serve with prosciutto on top. Prosciutto crudo and melon is an Italian dish that is amazing to consume as a light lunch on a summer day.

The leftover melon that you put in the fridge, you can keep it until you feel like having a smoothie. Smoothies are super easy to make. Just add frozen fruit to milk or yoghurt and voila, you got yourself a smoothie. We like to make sweet summer smoothies, so we take the melon out of the freezer and add them to our smoothie maker. If you don't have a smoothie maker you can just use a good mixer or a mixing stick. Add some milk, but don't add too much at the beginning, since you can always add a little more at the end if you see that the texture is too thick. Add a scoop of vanilla ice cream, 2 spoons of Greek yoghurt and we also add a bit of our berry bubbles or strawberry fun. It gives it a beautiful colour and adds to the sweetness.

## Spice flowers

Nasturtium is a climbing plant with beautiful flowers. There are different varieties and colours but they are all edible, the leaves and the flowers. They are incredibly healthy; both the leaves and the flowers have high amounts of vitamin C and they are great at improving the immune system, preventing and curing colds and infections.

**How to grow it:** You can buy the dried seeds from a garden centre or if you already have a plant, you will see small, green round seeds at the end of the stem. If they fall off once you touch them, they are ready to be dried and planted. Dry them for a few days on a window sill and once they look like light brown raisins, you can plant them in a pot. Nasturtiums are climbing plants but they also do very well in a normal pot or in the garden. They grow almost anywhere if they are exposed to a lot of sun.

**How to use it:** The taste is slightly spicy; you can use the flowers to decorate your salads and to give it a little kick. Or you can make a spicy dip. In order to make the dip, you will need around 20 leaves or flowers. Wash them in a bowl of cold water and dry them. Place them in your blender, add a clove of fresh garlic, some chopped onion, some chilli flakes if you like it extra spicy, some vinegar and olive oil. Don't add too much liquid at the beginning so that you can first see the consistency. You can always make it more liquid later by adding more olive oil.

Blend it until you have a smooth consistency. You can add some salt and pepper at the end. You can use the dip on top of vegetables, fish or even mix it inside your pasta. You can also use the flowers to make yourself a healthy tea. Just put a few flowers in your glass and pour hot water over it – it is especially great if you are fighting a cold.

# Apple Treats

'An apple a day keeps the doctor away'. Apples are filled with fibres and antioxidants. They are linked to lowering the risk of many health issues, like diabetes, heart disease and cancer.

How to grow it: You could grow an apple from an apple seed that you extract from an organic apple, but before your tree will be big enough and produce apples, you will have to wait a few years. If you want to do so, you need to carefully cut the apple without damaging the seeds. Each apple has around ten seeds. Let them dry for two to three days and plant them in your garden around 5 millimetres deep. You will have to do this in the fall if you want to succeed. Be generous with the seeding since only a few will actually grow into a tree. Another option is to just buy a small apple tree in a garden centre and plant it directly into your garden. There are also mini apple trees that could survive in a pot on your balcony and give you apples. The nice thing about having an apple tree in your garden is that the apple tree will bloom with beautiful white flowers. If you don't have the space or you don't want to wait three years to have apples, just buy a few apples at your grocery store.

How to use it: 'Once you have your apples, give them a quick wash and take out the centre with an apple corer. Prepare an oven tray and pieces of aluminium foil that are big enough to cover the apple completely. Now you can start with the filling.

Melt a spoon of butter and mix it with the juice of half a lemon. Add a spoon of brown sugar, a spoon of almond flour and raisins, mix it all together and fill it into the centre hole of the apple. Now wrap the apple with the aluminium foil and put them on your oven tray. Leave them in the oven and use a long toothpick or a knife to check if they are soft for about fifteen to twenty minutes. This recipe is amazing because you can use it if you go camping. You can bring your prepared apples in aluminium foil, and bake them like you would with a potato on the open fire.

# Herb Mix

'Herbs are essential for medicine, aromas and to give more flavour to your food. Each herb has a different taste and different benefits. There are around three thousand different types of herbs, but the most common are: chives, rosemary, thyme and oregano. Chives helps to fight inflammation, rosemary improves the blood circulation, thyme helps to fight fungal infections and oregano prevents cell damage.

**How to grow it:** You can find small pots with herbs, even in a bigger grocery store. They are super easy to keep, since you just need to water them every few days and keep them close to a window so that they can get enough sun. The best part of herbs is that you can use it straight away, and you don't need to wait till they bloom or fruit. When you harvest your herbs don't cut more than a third of your plant, so that the plant can stay healthy and it can grow back.

**How to use it:** Herbs can be used in anything, but the best usage is to make your own herb butter, which you can use on bread or let it melt on top of a nice steak. Herb butter is also very easy to make. Take out butter from the fridge and let it get soft. Then you add the herbs you desire and mix it. But if you want it more sophisticated, you need to start by roasting garlic. Take a whole garlic – yes not a clove but the whole garlic. When roasted, it will lose the garlic taste and become more nutty, so you don't have to worry about garlic breath. Cut off the back part so that the cloves are exposed and pour some olive oil over it. Wrap it into some aluminium foil and put it in the 200 °C preheated oven until your biggest clove is soft, which will take around forty to fifty minutes. In the meantime, you can cut your herbs. We use chives, since that's the biggest plant we had in our garden, but you can pick the one you like best. Cut the herb in super small pieces and put it in a bowl together with the soft butter. Once your garlic is ready and soft, you can use a knife to take out the cloves out of the garlic and add them to the butter mixture. Now you need to mix everything together and you will have an amazing roasted garlic herb butter that you can put back in the fridge, or in the freezer if you want to preserve it for a longer time. It is great to use on top of a steak, a baked potato or even on a toast with a fried egg on top.

# Leek Light

Leek has many health benefits; they help with your digestion, they promote weight loss, reduce inflammation and heart diseases, and they may lower your blood sugar levels.

**How to grow it:** Leeks are incredible, so you can always plant them. They will even survive a frosty winter, giving you a healthy meal while it's cold outside. You will need a garden to plant them, since they don't do so well in pots. Buy leek seeds and plant them in small pots. Since the seeds are small don't cover them with too much soil at the start. Keep the pot moist until the seeds germinate. Once they are 15 to 20 centimetres long, you can move them into the garden. Dig a hole in the soil and plant the leek, if you want to plant more than one, then keep them 15 centimetres apart from each other. When you put the small leeks in the holes and pour water over them, there is no need to cover it up with soil if your hole is small, so that the leek has the space to grow wider. Once your leeks are big, they are ready to be harvested.

**How to use it:** If you don't have a garden to plant leeks, you can buy some leeks at the grocery store for the recipe. Cut the leek into 1 centimetre pieces, wash them in cold water and dry them. Put a wok pan on the stove, and put in a bit of butter, a splash of olive oil and a spoon of mild curry.

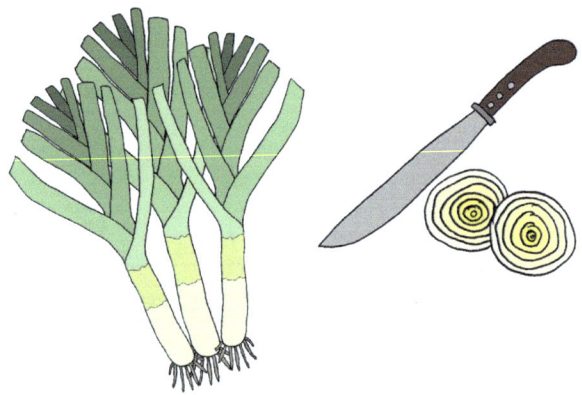

Let it all mix while heating up. Add the leek slices and some stem ginger syrup. Now reduce the heat to medium and cover your wok pan with a lid for ten minutes – and ready is your leek light. If you want to add a finishing touch, you can add some mascarpone or some coconut milk to give it that extra flavour.

# Onion Queen

Onion is the queen of all vegetables; you can generally use onion in almost every dish. It is incredibly healthy since it can protect against blood clots and it may help to reduce high blood pressure, and it fights whatever cold or infection you have.

**How to grow it:** Onion is one of those vegetables that you can grow from the leftovers of your cooking. You cut one quarter of the back part of your onion and take off the peel to avoid that part to rot. Take a jar that is a little smaller than your onion, fill it with water and lay the onion on top. Make sure that the roots are in the water. Leave them in a sunny place and in three days, you should already see some new white roots. Change the water every two to three days and in ten days you should be able to see something green coming out of your onion, that means that they are ready to be planted. Take the onion and lay it on rich moist soil. Cover the white onion part with a bit of soil but leave the green new growth exposed. After two weeks you should see the onion grow. The onion will also flower and once the flower dies off you can take little black seeds out of the flower. And a few months later, you should be able to see the new bulbs on the bottom or the stem. Those are your new onions that are ready to be harvested.

**How to use it:** You can use onion in literally everything, to cook meat or fish, to put it in your salad or to make a dip. But the best usage for onion is onion marmalade. "Onion marmalade?" you ask? Yes, onion marmalade is amazing with every meat dish, on top of a fancy cheese platter, or inside of your burger. In order to make onion marmalade you need to have four to five big onions. The best are red onions, since they are sweeter.

Cut them in thin slices and put them in a cooking pot. Pour 2 spoons of olive oil over it and add some salt and pepper. Let them cook with a lid on the pot and stir every now and then. Let the juices of the onion steam to soften the onion. Once the onions are a bit translucent, you need to add 5 spoons of brown or white sugar, 2 spoons of balsamic vinegar and half a cup of red wine. Reduce the heat to low and let it simmer covered with the lid for two to three hours, without forgetting to steer it occasionally. If your onions are dark brown and really soft, and there is no liquid left in the pot, then your onion queen marmalade is ready. You can put it straight inside of a burger, add it to a fancy cheese plate or put it in a sterilised jar. When you put it in a jar, put on the lid, flip the jar upside down and let it cool off. Once cooled off you will be able to keep it for around six months inside a dark cupboard. Once you open the jar you will need to leave it in the fridge.

# Apricot Pop

Apricots are amazing for promoting eyesight, since they contain carotene. It also contains a lot of vitamin A, which helps to regenerate your cells.

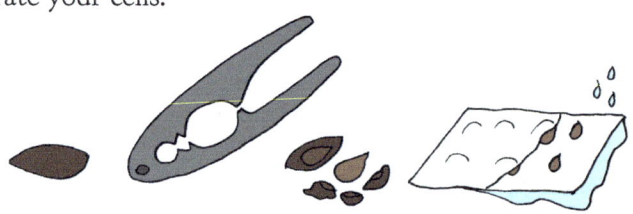

**How to grow it:** In order to grow apricots, you will need a garden, since the apricot tree can grow pretty big. You can even grow a whole tree from the seed of an organic store-bought apricot. You will need to break open the apricot nut to take out the seed and leave it for a week in wet kitchen paper until you see something grow, which means that it's sprouting. After that, you plant it in a small pot, and once it grows a bit you can plant it in the garden. In case you don't have a garden or you don't have enough space in it, you can just buy a few apricots for this recipe.

**How to use it:** Take 3 or 4 apricots, remove the seed in the centre and put the pulp in the blender. Add a splash of water or orange juice if you need to make it more fluid. It should have the consistency of a smoothie. Then add 2 Greek yoghurts. You can use any yoghurts to be honest, but the Greek yoghurt is best, since it is thicker, and will not leak as much when you take it out of the freezer during a hot summer. Mix your fruits with the yoghurt – you don't need to mix it too well, since it will look nicer if it has a marble look. And now you are ready to freeze it. The easiest way is to wash out the yoghurt cups so that you can recycle them into ice cream containers, or just use a paper cup. Pour your mixture inside the recycled containers and cover it with aluminium foil. Put a wooden ice cream stick inside, through the centre of the foil. The aluminium foil will make sure that your popsicle will be centred. Put it in the freezer and within a few hours you have a lovely homemade apricot popsicle. Of course, you can also do it without the wooden stick, and scoop the ice cream out later.

## Tomato Tuesday

There are ten thousand different tomato varieties. They come in different sizes, shapes and colours. Red tomatoes are the most common, but you can also find them in green, pink, yellow and black. The taste also varies, some are sweeter and some are more salty. Tomatoes, besides being great in a salad, are also filled with vitamins, and they say that they also reduce the risk of heart diseases and cancer.

**How to grow it:** if you are a first-time tomato cultivator then don't go for the green variety, since it will be harder to recognise when they are ripe. The easiest is to buy a small plant from a garden centre and plant it straight into a bigger pot once you are home. Water it as soon as you have planted it. Tomato is quite easy since the leaves will start hanging if you didn't water it enough, so just look at the leaves and it will tell you what it needs.

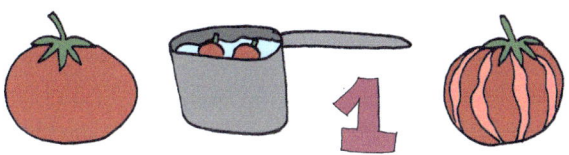

**How to use it:** You can slice them and use them to make a caprese salad, or a normal seasonal salad. If you have a lot of them, you could make your own tomato pasta sauce which you can keep in your kitchen cupboard for when you don't feel like cooking. You can just make pasta and heat up your sauce. Within ten minutes you will have a healthy spaghetti pomodoro. In order to make your Tomato Tuesday sauce, you need to peel around five to seven tomatoes, depending on their size. The easiest way is to boil some water in a cooking pot and put the tomatoes in for ten seconds, and then put them in a bowl of really cold water immediately after extracting them from the pot. The skin of the tomato will burst open and you can peel off the skin easily. Take the seeds out with a spoon and cut them in pieces.

Now cut an onion and prepare a cooking pot with some olive oil inside. Add the pieces of onion to the pan and let them turn into a golden colour. Add 700 grams of minced meat, some salt and pepper, and wait till the meat is cooked. Once the meat is cooked you can add the tomatoes and some basilicum and oregano, and stir to mix everything together. Reduce the heat and let it sit for thirty minutes. But keep stirring every now and then. Ready is your tomato Tuesday, the only thing you need to do now is boil some pasta and plate it. First the pasta, then the Tomato Tuesday on top and if you also want to take an instagrammable photo, add 2 leaves of basilico on top.